The Accidental Karma

By

Glenn Wolkoff

Scientia Est Vox

The Accidental Karma
By
Glenn Wolkoff

Copyright © 2010 Glenn Wolkoff

Cover design by Glenn Wolkoff

Vitae Mind Publishing
C/o Glenn Wolkoff
4804 Laurel Canyon Blvd., #190
Valley Village, CA 91607
www.vitaemind.com

Sometimes I wonder if it's all a dream

If nothing really is or what I seem

To be is only thoughts going through my mind

And all the things I think are but a kind

Of motion picture that I watch and feel

Thinking the things that happen are really real

And if it's all a dream I wonder too

If I'm alone forever and if you

Are only figments of this dreamy thought

And only I exist in empty naught

Maybe I'm all alone asleep and still

Dreaming forever endlessly God's will

Eyvind Earle

We live in illusion,

And the appearance of things.

There is a reality.

We are that reality.

When you understand this,

You see that you are nothing.

And being nothing,

You are everything.

That is all.

Kalu Rinpoche

From the author

I have a way of making things happen and of unsticking people who are stuck. I speak frankly and make it easy for others to tell me honestly where they are in the process of life.

I have always been more an observer of life than a participant. I love knowledge, wisdom and truth. My view of the universe is one of an object of study. I am always searching for more knowledge.

My most profound discovery is so simple that I can hardly conceive that it took a lifetime to comprehend. I now know that the greatest things in life are accomplished in the lightest of heart.

I recently crossed paths with a person that told me my purpose in life is to validate and record what I know. I was told I need to write; that my observations are critical to the universe, and there will be people who come after me who need to know what I have to say. Most importantly, that people will learn who and what they are by reading my words. After hearing this, and after much contemplation, I began to write.

What I hope for is that people see the connectedness they have with each other, with nature, and with the universe. We need to discover what it is we can do each and every day that will make a difference in the universe.

Introduction

The intent of my first book, *The Power*, was to present the message that you are a spiritual being with a thinking mind having human experiences through a physical body. Your body is not who you are. Once you accept and understand this, you will discover you have the power do anything. You are given a gift when you are put here. All you have to do is accept who you are. Through the choices you make and the thoughts you hold, you can create anything. We do not live this way because we choose to not accept this as truth. Our lives are limited to that which we accept.

The Power also talked about you being "thinking energy." Everything is energy, including your thoughts. Energy and thought are what create the reality of the physical Universe. You also have "free will" which is the ability to choose. What you accept and the choices you make are what create the life you live. You have to make sure of one thing before exercising your freedom to choose; the basis of your decision must be based on truth.

Lastly, in _The Power_, I told you that you are Source and that your purpose in life is to fully evolve back to your origin of Source. It is because you are Source, that you are able to use your energy to turn conscious thought into physical reality. Consciousness accomplishes the rearrangement of form, inclusive of the self. You do this by being an observer; seeing what you want as if it already exists. Your true purpose in life is to be you! You need to learn, you need to evolve, and you need to create. And ultimately, you need to return to your true divine self that Source intends you to be.

If you look up "divine being" you will find the following definitions:

- Creator and ruler of the Universe;

- Ruling over all eternal spirit and infinite mind;

- A person of supreme value;

- One believed to have more than natural attributes and powers.

I agree that this is indeed a definition of divinity. It is also a definition of you, a definition of me, and a definition of every spiritual being walking this plane in the disguise of a human body. Because I know this to be the truth, I must wonder why we do not act divine.

We are not divine because we have been taught that divinity is something that exists external to us. This is one of the greatest deceptions taught to mankind! When mankind accepted this doctrine, they were stripped of their divine nature, and Source was taken out of the man. This deception places a limit on our spiritual growth and allows us to be controlled.

Once you accept the truth that you are Source, you will learn that everything is possible and that there is nothing you cannot do. When you acknowledge your spiritual nature, you will understand how thought and energy creates reality. Accept and embrace who you really are and create your own reality!

No one understood the relationship between energy, thought, and reality better than Yeshua ben Joseph. He had a mind so evolved that he could visualize what did not exist, then make it so. You can do the same! It's a matter of acceptance. You accomplish this by focusing on and seeing what you expect, rather than on what exists. Yeshua's reason for being here was to teach you the essence of your divine nature by showing you the connection between mind and matter. Yeshua also demonstrated for you that life is eternal and does not end with the death of the body. Your energy source exists with or without your body.

Science has made a remarkable observation in people who lose an arm or a leg. They continue to feel pain in the missing limb. Even though the physicality of the limb no longer exists, the energy of the limb seems to remain, and the energy of the missing limb is perceived as pain by the brain. Medical journals refer to this phenomenon as "phantom pain." This is the same as when your physical body no longer exists; your energy source continues to remain strong and alive.

This book is in many ways a continuation of my first book. So why karma? Because every event in your life is linked to a previous event. There are no results in life without a cause. Things do not just happen, and there are no coincidences.

Karma is a collection of all of your choices, actions, and non-actions that add up to your current state of being. With every action you take, you create energy. That energy creates a cause that will eventually find its way back to you with a corresponding effect. When actions are for the good sake of others, positive energy and good karma finds its way back to you. However; if you create bad karma through actions that are selfish and hurtful to others, you create a karmic debt owed.

I quote from Richard Bach's *Messiah's Handbook*, " If you want to meet someone who can fix any situation you don't like, who can bring you happiness in spite of what other people say or believe, look in the mirror, then say this magic word: Hello."

Table of Contents

Chapter 1:   Accidents

"For an accident to happen, one must plan and participate in the events that lead up to it."

Glenn Wolkoff

The next time you are walking down the street and a flower pot falls off a nearby balcony and hits you on the head, don't say "Why me?", but rather "Thank you...I must have deserved that!" And if you observe it happening to someone else, I suggest you offer aid.

There is no such thing as an accident!

It takes a lot of decision making and event participation for you to end up in any specific location at any specific moment.

Events happen because everything is constantly changing through the energy of both conscious creation and evolution. These continuous changes cause constant reactions in order to maintain balance and harmony in the Universe. Everything that materializes was once a thought that becomes an image as energy forms around the thought. Form in the material Universe is really solidified thought images and energy.

Every event in your life is an effect of a previous cause…cause and effect. Each experience you encounter in your life is a test of your evolutionary growth. Each decision you make sets up the next event and/or lesson to be learned. The results of the events that you experience are not as important as how you deal with the events. Most important is what you learn and understand from the events. Learning through experience is how you evolve.

If every material object is the result of an idea held in thought before its materialization, then why do things happen to you that you have never held in thought? Unfortunately, it is NOT necessarily YOUR thought intensity that creates the materialization. The Universe is full of people, full of thoughts, and full of energy.

The further you evolve, the more you create; but until you learn to give your ideas deliberate form, you will not have what you wish to create or experience. Events will suddenly occur without you knowing you had a need because the true need you desire is in your reaction to the event. You learn the most through your reactions and responses to events in your life.

The frequency of things happening to you that you attribute to being "accidental" is a good indication of your spirit's evolution. Think of unplanned events in your life as a test of measuring your reaction to them. No matter how serious they seem to be, there is a reason they happen, and that they happen to you. One of the fundamental rules of karma is that there are no results in life without a cause. Things do not just happen!

Always remember that life is a series of events and until the end of any one series is reached, you may not always know the meaning of any particular event in the causal chain. This is why it is so important that you focus your energies on your reaction and response rather than on the event itself. Focusing on the event itself creates a situation of being stuck in time and space. You always want to respond and move on.

No effect can happen without a preceding cause to account for it. It is always a consequence of an occurrence. All choices you make in life are the beginning of a flow of consequences. It is always part of the causal chain. You are also part of the causal chain. Because you did not contemplate the result, you may mistakenly believe that it occurred by accident.

Events that occur regularly and constantly according to the physical laws of the Universe are never a result of chance. They may be unintended from your perspective, but they are not unforeseen in the Universe. They are random, but rather purposeful by design.

There is always conscious thought behind the natural force of any occurrence in the Universe. People today tend to attribute more and more of the events in their life as accidents. The truth of the matter behind this is a false sense of no control over life because the Universe is becoming more fragmented and dispirited.

Chapter 2:   Karma

"Karma is the sum of the whole; a collection of all of your choices, actions, and non-actions that when added together, equal your current state of being."

Glenn Wolkoff

"There is a wonderful mythical law of nature that the three things we crave most in life---happiness, freedom, and peace of mind---are always attained by giving them to someone else."

Peyton Conway March

"How people treat you is their karma; how you react is yours."
"When you judge another, you don't define them, you define yourself."

Dr. Wayne Dyer

Karma is the Sanskrit word for "action." Sanskrit is a sacred language used in the philosophy of both Hinduism and Buddhism. Conceptually, it is the total effect of your actions and conduct that determines outcomes in successive phases of your existence. It is the eternal law of the spirit that is more commonly known as "What goes around comes around." It really is all about the universal law of "cause and effect." In more simple terms, you are what you have been. Your karma determines your current state of being because of the energy created through your thoughts and actions.

The driving force behind karma is the principle that every action has an equal and opposite reaction. Every time we think something, speak something or do something, we create a cause, which will eventually have a corresponding effect. The cycle of cause and effect defines your existence.

Since results are similar to the cause, positive causes create the effect of happiness, and negative causes create the effect of suffering. This is a simple, but often forgotten rule. You also need to understand that once an action is done, the result is never lost, even if it does not immediately occur. Although you may not have experienced an effect you caused, it is still out there; it never disappears.

What you have done to others creates a cause, or in other words, an agreement of a next effect. Many of these agreements are formed and experienced throughout your life based on karmic justice.

Because all people are responsible for their own acts and thoughts; each person's karma is their own doing. In order to achieve good karma, you must live life doing what is right. Good karma contributes to how rewarding your next incarnation will be.

You learn life lessons at your own pace as you journey through all of your incarnations. The only way you can take control of your karma is by accepting responsibility in your life. Because of karma, you cannot escape the consequences of your actions.

There are three basic types of acts that make up your karma:

    (1) acts which are for the benefit of others or selfless;

    (2) acts which focus on gains for oneself or selfish; and

    (3) acts taken spontaneously, without any thought of consequences.

Ancient scriptures talk about the importance of self-discipline so that one promotes acts solely for the benefit of others. Living life through the first type of selfless act leads to the salvation of the spirit. Living life through the second and third acts is connected to the physical rather than the spiritual. We experience all traits and emotions in the physical Universe through our separate self. We then need to relinquish these experiences to return to our true higher self.

So…karma is created by thoughts, words and actions. It lives inside your consciousness, and it stays with you each time you incarnate. There are many problems that appear in our society because people do not understand the concept of karma, and do not understand that their life is defined, not by the events that happen to them, but rather how they react to those events.

If you live an honest good life, follow the path of truth, and do right by others, then good karma will come your way. If you follow a life of deception and delusion, and bring harm to others, then karmic debt will find you. Karma provides you with a goal of becoming a better spirit by learning from your life experiences. Think of karma as a bank account with positive (good) and negative (bad) karma being accumulated. The purpose of the karma is to balance the energies deposited.

It is a process that teaches us the lessons of evolution. Passing your lessons is what allows you to further evolve in life. You are the master of your Universe; you determine your life through the choices you make and how you live. Your current state of being is exactly what you chose it to be.

Each of us is a spiritual being who incarnates in the physical Universe many times in order to evolve toward a greater state of consciousness. During this evolutionary path of incarnations, you accumulate wisdom, and make wise choices that benefit your next incarnation. You may also make incorrect choices that create a burden in your next incarnation. You take on your burdens to learn a lesson that you previously failed to learn. These burdens are known as karmic debt. This will be discussed further in the next chapter.

You are here to evolve. What you learn most through your wanderings in the Universe is that life is simply a journey of choices. Through the trial of many lifetimes, you will experience all things....fame and insignificance; wealth and poverty; sickness and wellness; victim and perpetrator; woman and man; different races; different religions, etc. The more you understand and learn through your experiences, the more you evolve. The only way to understand what it is to be these things is to experience them through a physical lifetime. You agree to these lessons each time you come here. Learning your lessons is what allows you to evolve. Because you have free will and you have intention, karmic consequences come your way to teach you something about things you have thought, spoken or done.

In every moment of your life, there are lessons for you to experience and learn from. There are too many lessons to learn and master in a single incarnation. That is why you are here over and over again. How you have treated others in previous incarnations is how you will be treated in next incarnations. It is an internal spiritual system of being held accountable for your actions. Hurting others creates bad karma and doing things to benefit others creates good karma.

If you have been imprisoned in this life for something you did not do, you can be certain that you have done something equally wrong in a past incarnation that you got away with. Karma knows no boundaries of time. Also, this is never done to punish. Karma does not punish. Likewise, karma does not reward for good acts. Karma is all about teaching the wisdom of life so that you learn to further evolve.

As we move through our lifetimes, we discover that the secret of our learning is directly linked to our discipline in pursuing it. T.S. Eliot said, "We shall not cease from exploration and the end of all our exploring will be to arrive where we started…and know the place for the first time."

Each time you incarnate, you become more aware of who and what you are. You look in a mirror and see yourself deeper than the eye can see, more precisely than the mind can know, and more compassionately than the heart can feel. More and more you come to understand that you are a spirit having a human experience rather than a human having a spiritual experience.

I will remind you again that the effect of karma, whether it is good or bad, is never a judgment, nor is it given as a reward or as punishment.

Understand that all things must eventually return to a balance in the Universe. Any movement created in the flow of life must also create a return to equilibrium somehow, somewhere. Because of that, the concept of justice is never postponed.

The Universe becomes a multiplication table full of equations that determine how to balance all causes with effects. All of the causes you have created will return to you as an effect to balance the equation. Every secret...every crime...every virtue...every wrong...is addressed. This universal process of balance is a necessity by which every part once again becomes a whole.

No sooner than you choose or act according to a particular course, there are results realized in it. You live in the flow of causation from which you cannot escape even for a moment...your life is moving from moment to moment...and these moments become the basis of moral and spiritual freedom to reach purity.

Because the law of karma is based on cause and effect, it impacts everything and everyone in the Universe. There is no escaping it...or is there? Some say that once you become enlightened, you no longer have or need karma, because at the point of enlightenment, the effects of karma are no longer necessary. Everything that an enlightened one does, says or thinks is through free will or a manifestation of their true and basic nature, and NOT the effect of past karma.

So, does an enlightened person escape from this process? From a moral causation point of view, yes you do. Your actions are no longer impacted by karma because you become united with it. The enlightened person is at one with the law of causation. Your karmic cycle is complete.

Karma is not a static, linear series of causes and effects. There is always the possibility of change driven through the attainment of wisdom. You can only reach enlightenment, when you become wise enough to no longer need these lessons to learn from. At that point, you have returned to your basic nature of origination. So in a sense, you do not escape karma, but rather, you become it. This is the emergence from one's self…a full realization of truth…and a full evolution back to Source.

To make it simple, think of good karma as energy you accumulate for giving out love to others and for opening yourself up to receive love from others. The more you do this, the more you are surrounded by positive energy. It works on an individual level, in groups of people, and even at a nationwide level when all thoughts are aligned for the better good of mankind. This is why it is so important that one day we have a positive united consciousness for all mankind.

If the balancing of all mankind's karma starts to err on the negative, you will begin to see global karma make itself felt through acts of nature and disease. This happens as a result of love, compassion and spirituality becoming scarce amongst us. On the other hand, if all mankind can return to its true nature of divinity, and act as such, problems in the Universe will start to correct themselves through a united positive consciousness.

I am reminded of an old poem that talks about asking for things and being told "no" because learning, understanding, and evolving is the only path to those things.

When you ask for strength, you are given difficulties to make you strong.

When you ask for wisdom, you are given problems to solve.

When you ask for prosperity, you are given brawn and brain to work.

When you ask for courage, you are given dangers to overcome.

When you ask for patience, you are placed in situations where you must learn to wait.

When you ask for love, you are given troubled people to help.

When you ask for favors, you are given opportunities.

When you ask to take away bad habits, you are told that they are yours to give up.

When you ask to make your handicapped child whole, you are told their spirit is whole, and that their body is only temporary.

When you ask for happiness, you are given blessings and told happiness is up to you.

When you ask to make your spirit grow, you are told you must learn to grow it yourself.

When you ask for material things so you may enjoy life, you are told you were given life so that you may enjoy material things.

You receive nothing, but you are given everything!

Chapter 3: Karmic Debt

"When you enter life, you are given two buckets; one full of positive energy, and one empty of negative energy. Karmic debt occurs when you take energy out of the positive bucket and deposit it into the negative bucket."

Glenn Wolkoff

"Like any debt owed in life, it takes hard work and positive efforts to pay it back."

Glenn Wolkoff

"People pay for what they do, and still more, for what they have allowed themselves to become. And they pay for it simply; by the lives they lead."

Edith Wharton

The common philosophy behind karmic debt is that whatever you do to someone in a past life, you will experience in a present life. There will come a moment and a place in your life to repay a karmic debt. The effect may be physical, emotional, mental or spiritual. The repayment of major karmic debts will occur when you are evolved spiritually. Why? Because, as an evolved spirit, you will be better able to handle serious karma with greater understanding and wisdom.

Think of karmic debt as a negative cause still looking for its effect. What this means is that you have misappropriated energies in a past life, yet the life cycle of that event has not yet returned to you. You have not yet been presented with an opportunity to learn the necessary lesson resulting from your wrongdoing. In essence, it is a life debt still owed.

Karmic debt is always negative energy that will eventually be returned to you when you least expect it. However, I will let in on a secret: if you demonstrate through good deeds that you have learned your lesson, you may be able to offset the debt before another event occurs.

Always remember that the purpose of karmic debt, like the purpose of karma, is to teach you a lesson in becoming a better person. I will keep repeating this; karma does not reward good behavior and it does not punish bad behavior. That being said, most people don't see it that way.

Sometimes people place karmic debt on themselves because they believe they are responsible for someone's negative outcome, when in reality, the reason for the outcome was caused by the other person making inappropriate choices in life. It is important that you recognize these situations to avoid self-imposed suffering that you do not deserve. You can simply release yourself from these debts by understanding that they do not belong to you.

Can you eradicate karmic debts? Eradication is possible, but very difficult. For complete eradication, you have to reach the highest spiritual level of consciousness; enlightenment. However, you can achieve partial eradication through letting go of all attachments, ill will, and negative emotions. This can also be achieved through acts of helping others. Meditation can be very helpful in the process of letting go of things. Additionally, you can lessen the effect of your debts or postpone your debts to another moment in life through the acts of asking for forgiveness and forgiving yourself.

You must always strive to develop yourself in spiritual growth through all of your physical incarnations in order to transcend all karma and its debts.

Your moments in the physical Universe are meant to be spent experiencing life and learning your life lessons. It's okay to play in the playground of the physical Universe; however, you will be held accountable for your actions through the consequences that follow you. These consequences carry over into each physical incarnation. With each repayment of a debt, you move forward with your spiritual evolvement.

Remember that karma creates learning situations for you; how you respond to these situations determines if debts get repaid or not. If you do not work through your debts, you do not get very far in your spiritual life.

Chapter 4:   Ends and Means

"When mankind accepts that the ends justify the means, we have taught our children that it makes no difference if you cheat on an exam or study hard for an exam so long as you get a good grade."

Glenn Wolkoff

"The first sign of corruption in a society that is still alive is that the end justifies the means."

Georges Bernanos

Throughout history, there has been much philosophical debate on the subject of ends and means. Does the end justify the means? A popular school of thought is that an act should be determined right or wrong strictly by its consequences. This is known as consequentialism. From a consequentialist point of view, a morally right action is one that produces a good outcome or consequence.

I do not accept this theory of thinking. From my perspective, the act itself should always be the determinant of right from wrong regardless of the outcome. This theory of belief is known as deontology.

The age old debate goes on today whether an end can justify a means. I often hear people say (as they wipe their brow), "Lucky me…that turned out okay." So, one must ask, can it sometimes be right to use any means to achieve a good end?

If we embrace the philosophy that a means can be right only in relation to an end, then we choose to justify life through the outcomes produced, rather than by how one gets there. This seems to be quite common today. The ultimate goal becomes accomplishing the purpose intended. If the intended purpose is the correct result, it can be concluded that the means was proper.

Let's think about this for a moment. My purpose is to pass a necessary exam for a job I want. With that end in mind, I determine that certain things will definitely help me to succeed and others may not. I may buy the answers to the exam or find another way to cheat on the exam. These methods may be appropriate when measured against the sole purpose to achieve my goal of passing the exam. After all, that is a good outcome. However, from a moral point of view, is taking any steps that might serve to accomplish my end correct? If not, then I would not be morally justified in employing such means even though the intended end was accomplished.

This is easy to understand when the end is good. However, what if the end is bad? A bad end is one that we are not morally justified in seeking; therefore, we should not be morally justified in taking any steps toward its accomplishment. No means can be justified by a bad end. Although this seems logical, another question to ask is what if all of your means were morally good acts but the end result was still bad? That in itself should not make your means incorrect.

This really brings us to the dilemma of the matter. When you use the ends to justify the means, it really fails to apply an appropriate standard to the means used. No matter how the end turns out, it cannot be used to justify the morality of the actions taken to get there.

Let's talk a little more about good ends. We should always be justified in working for their accomplishment. However, that does not mean that we are also morally justified in using any means to get there. Fundamental philosophy argues that if the end is really good, and if the means really serves the end, then there can be nothing wrong with the means. It is justified by the end, and we are justified in using it. So, if I want to be a surgeon in order to save people's lives and I achieve that goal by cheating my way through medical school, the end for me is really good. I am a surgeon! The means I used really did serve the end of being a surgeon. However, this end will not turn out to be so good for the patients I perform surgery on.

For most of us, it should begin to become clear that life is not about "ends" but rather the "means" we use to accomplish things. None of the arguments are morally correct when you use the ends to justify the means. Nor should you use means to justify ends. Every act you perform should be morally correct independent of everything else!

There is still one more argument out there that says that a good end can never result unless the means are also good. If an action is morally bad in itself, it cannot really serve a good end, even though it may on the surface appear to do so. So, if I cheat on my exam and achieve the good end of passing the exam, then my cheating becomes okay because only a good means can achieve a good end? Or are we saying that passing the exam is really not a good end because I cheated? It just appears to be a good end. Imagine living life through this thinking process.

I will leave you with an interesting question to consider. Is telling a lie that has no negative affect on anyone or that spares someone hurt feelings a good thing? We all too often kid ourselves by the statement that the end justifies the means.

Simplify life and measure every act, independent of everything else, to be morally correct!

Chapter 5:   Free Will

Those who believe free will does not exist stand still on the tracks as the train approaches; those who know better step aside to safety."

Glenn Wolkoff

"For all of us who are alive, life is the real issue. Yet so often we judge our existence by the things that happen to us—by whether things are going our way or not. Sometimes we feel strong—strong enough to dictate our future. Sometimes we feel that we can make things happen. Then there are times when we feel totally helpless. But through all the dramas and bumps, there is life. There is the very powerful, very existence of every single human being."

Prem Rawat

I find it very disconcerting to read about all the philosophical theories and science based theories out there that deny the existence of free will.

Without free will, there is no morality and without morality there is no being held responsible for one's actions. Are we really supposed to believe that this is the way life works?

The freedom of the will has been one of the most difficult challenges in past literary works. The arguments arise out of the idea of *determinism.*

The determinism argument goes something like this:

All events and things have causes which are independent of their effects. Okay...I can accept that...it sounds like the basic cause and effect theory discussed throughout this book.

Determinism then goes on to say that for the will to truly be free, there must be no external influence, and that is not possible because every event has causes independent of itself. In science, it is agreed that all effects are rendered inevitable by their causes, and in morality, we try to find an exception to make some sense of all this.

I would argue that the necessary conditions for a free will are internal. We can observe human actions, but we cannot observe the will. A free will must come from an original power within us; a power that is truly our own.

Determinism concludes that since every event has a prior cause, we are not really free to choose, and therefore, cannot be held responsible.

The legal system has always decided whether or not a person acted freely AND also decided whether the will was free to form a requisite intent. The legal system figured out that we have something that is free to think on its own accord; we have a mind.

Of course, no one ever wants to talk about things that are not physical in nature. If you haven't already noticed...I love to!

We have a thinking mind that allows us to make independent decisions on how to act regardless of the conditions we are confronted with. Events that happen are not in our control; however, the choices we make in reaction to those events are ALWAYS one of free will. Therefore, we are always accountable for our actions.

The mind goes through a process of deliberation….because it consists of thinking energy…..and is free to act on its own.

I will be the first to admit that everything depends on everything else. Our existence at any given moment is dependent on everything else in the Universe. Everything in the Universe is connected through the energy of cause and effect. All people are connected through the same energy. All this means is that we cannot be held accountable for the events that happen to us.

HOWEVER, we are always accountable and responsible for how we decide to react to these events. We have free will to choose our own course of action.

We have the freedom to make right choices and we have the freedom to make wrong choices.

We are spiritual beings with thinking minds having human experiences through a physical body. Determinism and science can debate with me on that one!

There is also a philosophy based on Descartes that provides a model explanation for dualism. It goes like this:

1. It is **imaginable** that one's mind might exist without one's body, therefore
2. It is **conceivable** that one's mind might exist without one's body, therefore
3. It is **possible** one's mind might exist without one's body, therefore
4. **One's mind is a different entity from one's body**!

THEREFORE...the mind has the ability to think independently of all external sources (including the body). Free will is alive and well and full of energy!

What follows is an excerpt from my first book, *The Power*. It is from Chapter One titled, *The Power*, in which I define the greatest power in the Universe to be free will---the ability to choose.

"You control your thoughts and emotions through the realization that you are able to choose what you think and choose how you feel. Many of the thoughts and emotions you have are not your own, but ones that have been imposed upon you from your external environment. To truly be in control means to not be swayed by the conditions you find yourself in, because your state of being is never circumstance-dependent. It is an independent state of being; a state of your consciousness.

Everything in the Universe is energy. Words, thoughts, feelings are also energy. Actions are expressions of energy. You create your life and your destiny through the choices you make. If you are not happy, choose to be happy and then follow a path of actions to fulfill that desire. What you project is what comes your way."

This is what free will is!

There was a research project that lasted ten years at a cost of $2.5 billion looking for natural cures in the medical community. After the completion of the project, something very interesting was discovered. It can be explained in two words; "I believe."

The medical community calls it "the placebo effect" — the ability of a sugar pill or a pretend treatment to make people feel better, just because they expect that it will. It's the mind's ability to alter physical symptoms.

Ten years and $2.5 billion to conclude what can be found on page one of the book of life!

The study showed that the placebo effect had demonstrated its healing powers. About a third of patients felt better when they received sugar pills instead of the intended actual drug.

The study concluded that many of the results of certain alternative procedures are largely placebo effects, unless you believe there are people who exert magical powers so they can hold their hands over your body and cure you of disease. Of course that is entirely possible, especially if you believe it.

It was discovered that the placebo effect could raise pulse rates, blood pressure and reaction speed when people were told they had taken a stimulant; the opposite occurred when people were told that a drug would make them drowsy. Brain imaging shows that beliefs can cause biological changes that affect levels of chemical messengers and stress hormones that signal pain or pleasure.

However, science is not willing to admit or conclude that the something that makes "I believe" work is the mind, and not the brain, which is physical in nature. From a scientific perspective, that makes sense because you can measure and record the brain and its activity. Energy and the mind, however, are a bit more challenging to analyze.

The brain is the command center of the physical body, but what is the command center of the brain? Like a computer, it thinks only because it has been programmed how to think. The brain thinks because it is told what to do from the mind. However, the mind is not physical, so science is challenged in studying and measuring it.

I also came across another study that talked about the "baby boomer" generation likely to be less healthy than their parent's generation. 78 million baby boomers entering their 60s may end up suffering from more disabilities than that age group from previous generations.

Research has found that those now entering their 60s are more likely to have disabilities such as falling as a result of immobility, urinary incontinence, memory loss and dementia, arthritis, high blood pressure, heart disease, osteoporosis and diabetes. The data was gathered from studies performed over the last two decades.

The concern of course is the burden this will place on both society and the health care system. The study attributes a large portion of the problem to obesity which is directly attributed to this generation being introduced to processed food.

Because healthy people in their 60s often still work and contribute to the economy, it is concerning that many of this age group will be disabled. That can lead to an economic downfall.

Unfortunately, science is missing the point! Just because processed food was introduced to this generation, no one mandated that it had to be our main source of nourishment. That is a behavioral issue directly attributed to the choices we make.

I also have a theory of my own regarding the physical health of this population. I hesitate to mention it and I will not elaborate on it because it will most likely not sit well with people.

This generation is also the one that has been introduced to the technology of computers, cell phones, and other such devices which I believe are changing the energy frequencies that surround us.

Since everything is energy, including us, and we use that energy (positive and negative) to either heal ourselves or damage ourselves; interruptions in the energy flow cause disturbances in our well-being. The energy around us, like processed food, is no longer natural because of all this technology sharing our fields of energy. The use of this technology has also caused us to be much less active and physical in our everyday life.

Don't misunderstand; technology offers us remarkable opportunities in life when used appropriately. These devices were intended to be tools that enhance life, not replace it. As always, it is our choice to decide how to us these devices and what impacts they have in our life.

It is a horrific thought to think that the next war could be one that unites all nations because we will not be fighting each other, but rather the enemy will be disease and illness. Disease is becoming one of the greatest threats to mankind.

In plain and simple terms; the condition of the Universe at this very moment is exactly what mankind has determined it to be. It is our doing. It is our creation. It is our manifestation through all of our compiled thoughts, actions and behavior.

Free will allows us to think what we want, to do what we want, and to behave as we want. Putting blame on anything external to ourselves is merely an excuse. The Universe belongs to us. It is ours to do with what we please.

If we want to change the Universe, we need to start exercising our power of free will and start thinking good thoughts. These thoughts cannot be based on individual needs; they need to be universal---all mankind thinking as one. If we all have our own agendas, the outcomes will be one against another. If we all think together, the outcomes will be in the best interest of mankind.

When I come across statistics like 7.7 million children dying annually before their 5th birthday (including 3.5 million from diarrhea and pneumonia), I have to wonder what's wrong with this great Universe we live in. These things are easily solved at minimal costs, yet they exist. Do we not care? If we do care, why do they exist?

People have the ability to think freely, act kindly, and fix the problems of the Universe we live in yet we tend to become deaf, blind and dumb when it comes to statistics like this. The majority of our actions are spent on our self and our immediate family. For the most part, the Universe is not our concern. However, when the Universe stops giving us what we need to care for our self or our immediate family, we certainly find the time to complain and criticize.

Mankind has the power to do anything it wants, yet for the most part, we focus on our own personal agendas. It does you no good to have everything you want when you live in a Universe that is unraveling from disease, hunger, lack of education, and economic crisis. It is this very type of selfish behavior that creates the conditions that will eventual take from us that which we seek.

Perhaps someday when people have evolved to be very wise, they will not need to see. I say this because we are blinded by what we see. We see the outside and not the inside. We see a male and a female, but not a person. We see the color of the skin, the shape of the body, but not the mind. We see physicality, but we are ignorant of spirit. We need to understand that all people are the same. All people come from the same source. People tend to believe that only what they see is real.

Physical existence is transitory; therefore, it is constantly changing. Your body limits you because it is physical in nature. Your spirit has unlimited capability. The spirit lives with or without your body. It is your spirit and your mind that give you your freedom in life. Your mind is what controls everything. It is your mind that allows you free will. Free will is your gift to choose what you want in life. You have the power to choose every thought you think. You have the power to choose every word you speak. You have the power to choose every action you take. Don't waste this gift. Use it! And, use it wisely!

Since your mind is the most important determinant of your well-being, use your free will to do the right things and your life will improve. Use your free will to help others and your life will improve. Use your free will to help the Universe you live in and your life will improve. When you choose to not exercise your free will to do these things, you choose to be a victim of circumstance. You choose to limit the power of your mind. If you do not believe in free will, then you have no power to accomplish anything. Lack of belief in free will leads to lack of belief in one's self. Once that occurs, you begin to do things that are self-destructive.

Your mind will never leave you. It does not perish. It is eternal. It existed before your body and it will exist after your body is gone. When people begin to act in the best interest of mankind rather than the best interest of self, the power of a united consciousness will eliminate poverty, hunger, disease, and ignorance. We must be mindful and conscious of everything and everyone.

Your mind knows no limitations; however, it lives in a physical Universe full of limitations. You need to focus on your inner self rather than the daily events performed by the outer self. Do not give away your power of free will through fear, or worry, or lack of decision making. You always end up with what you think, so pay close attention to your thoughts.

The Universe may be going bankrupt in a material sense; however, the time for true concern is when mankind begins to go bankrupt in a spiritual sense. Life is an experience. We were meant to live happy lives, and were meant to have all of our needs met. I did say "needs", not wants. If you need a better life, you must discover your inner self. It is your divine nature that will change your life and change the Universe you live in.

One of my favorite quotes from Yeshua ben Joseph is one that few people know:

"When you make the two into one, when you make the inner like the outer and the outer like the inner, and the upper like the lower, when you make male and female into a single one, so that the male will not be male and the female will not be female, when you make eyes replacing an eye, a hand replacing a hand, a foot replacing a foot, and an image replacing an image, then you will enter the kingdom. Therefore, if one is unified, one will be filled with light, but if one is divided one will be filled with darkness."   ---From the Gospel of Thomas

There is more to life than what you see. Appreciate what you have. Love everything and everyone around you, and let them love you. Think and act in the best interest of mankind and the Universe rather than just yourself. And, most importantly, use your power of free will to make life what you need it to be.

You have to always remember that you **experience** the physical Universe through your physical body. Experiencing the physical does not mean that you have to live in the physical. Physical needs are very little; nourishment, shelter, and movement. Since all that is rather boring, we supplement it with money, material belongings, and status. Those are all false needs. When you chase false needs in life, you will suffer and you will be unhappy.

Spiritual needs on the other hand are quite fascinating: energy, happiness, love, and wisdom. You can, of course, live in the physical Universe, but choose to chase spiritual fulfillment. Instead of focusing your life on your body, making as much money as you can, and owning everything you can; spend your life surrounding yourself with positive energy and thought, being happy, giving and receiving love, and acquiring wisdom through the lessons life teaches you. This is how you evolve. You will find that when you live life through a spiritual state of mind, you will have unlimited good health, unlimited happiness and fulfillment, and you will experience a life without suffering.

Best of all, you will be able to explore the joys of the physical with little or no limitations.

Me

by

Glenn Wolkoff

I woke up in the morning and my car was gone…

I woke up in the morning and my house was gone…

I woke up in the morning and my job was gone…

I woke up in the morning and my money was gone…

I woke up in the morning and my clothes were gone…

I woke up in the morning and my name was gone…

I woke up in the morning and my status was gone…

But I still woke up and I was still me!

I woke up in the morning and my energy was gone…

Me was able to replenish it from the Universe.

I woke up in the morning and my love was gone…

Me knew that if I loved myself, others would also love me.

I woke up in the morning and my spirit was gone…

Me was gone as well.

Chapter 6:   Source

"The true value of a human being is determined by the measure and the sense in which they have obtained liberation from the self. We shall require a substantially new manner of thinking if humanity is to survive."

Albert Einstein, 1954

"When you discover your true self, you will understand that you need nothing else."

Glenn Wolkoff

"I just refer to myself as being Spirit, Mind and Body like everyone else and working toward the mastery of my natural divinity and the healing of my emotional mind."

Leonard Orr

"Everyone has a spirit that can be refined, a body that can be trained in some manner, a suitable path to follow. You are here to realize your inner divinity and manifest your innate enlightenment."

Morihei Ueshiba

I talk a lot about Source, and people always ask me what Source is. **Source is who you truly are.** Source is your divine nature. Source is yours to do with whatever you want. Source can do anything. Source can create everything. You can do anything. You can create everything. Your life is determined by how you choose to use Source.

Source is energy....a generative force. It is a dynamic quality. It allows you the capacity to be active. As energy, it exists everywhere. It is everything....both physical and non-physical. It is your origin. It is where you come from. It is what you go back to. Source supplies you with information. It gives you everything you need to know. Because you are Source, you have a positive spiritual force that flows through your body.

We are here to create all that we can imagine. Source is not something independent of you. It is you. It is important that you understand that you are Source. Accept that you are Source! It is your spiritual nature and your thinking mind. You needed a physical body to experience the physical plane, so Source provided it for you. Source provides you with everything you need. You merely need to know how to ask. Source creates anything you can think. Because of Source, energy and thought create physical reality.

We create physical bodies for the sole purpose of experiencing physical life. Without a body, we could not experience what the senses offer us. We are curious beings. We love to create. There is only one rule of morality we have to abide by; create and do not destroy.

The body evolved very quickly in order to experience the physical senses. Because of that, we began to lose our divine nature. Eventually the body took charge, and we no longer existed as the divine creators we were. Instead, we existed as a body that would do anything to survive. The domination of the body's will to survive lessened our spiritual capabilities and placed limitations on our existence. Our awareness of Source becomes diminished when we are in a physical body.

Once we lost our divine nature, the body began to get sick with disease. This created fear in mankind, and once fear appeared, the death of the body was inevitable. With our divinity forgotten, mankind started to live a life based on both fear and survival. Physical existence became the focus of life. We have become so attached to the false self---the physical self---that we have forgotten who and what we are. One of the first things we must do to reclaim our divine nature is liberate ourselves from fear.

We have created a Universe that has placed such huge limitations on our existence that in essence, we have manifested a prison for ourselves. There is only one way out. We must return to our divine nature. We must go back to being the creators of our Universe.

The purpose of physical life is to create, experience life, and enjoy life. We were meant to come and go often. Somewhere along the way we fell into the trap of wanting to stick around in the physical for as long as possible, and at any cost. We were supposed to be here free from illness and disease, but because we have forgotten who we are, the physical body ages, gets sick, and dies.

We have the ability to manifest any thought that we hold in our consciousness. We also have the ability to live free from all illness. Unfortunately, when we turn the controls over to our physicality, none of these things happen.

I think that you will see more and more cases of what appears to be illness in people who understand that they can move on and leave their bodies behind rather than wait for their body to dictate their fate. People are suddenly disappearing from a perspective of thought and functionality leaving behind a healthy body with nobody home on the inside. Science believes this is caused by illness and comes up with labels and ways to treat it. I believe it is the result of very intentional conscious thoughts on the part of your spiritual self. The greater consciousness has figured out how to leave the body without experiencing death.

We have created a burden upon ourselves with the belief that we must die. It is beliefs like this that cause harm to mankind through manifested disease. Illness, and the fear of disease, has become one of the greatest threats to mankind.

We are all divine beings! In our natural state, love and healing will surround us. Our primary goal is to experience joy and love of self. Learn to heal, learn to forgive, and learn to manifest your dreams. Accept responsibility for what you are. Be a responsible creator. Remember that the physical Universe evolved from the spiritual Universe. When you become your spiritual self you affect the physical Universe. Be at one with your creation. The physical Universe is our imagination. Ideas taking form!

Because karma is stored in the astral (spiritual) body and causal (consciousness) body, it is essential that you recognize and understand your true nature. These astral and causal bodies follow you through each physical incarnation. This is why you cannot escape your karma until all life lessons have been learned, and enlightenment is obtained.

Like DNA being the coding that determines your physicality, Source and karma are the coding that determines your energetic body; your spiritual self. Source is your origin. Source is your completion. Source is the energy cycle of all creation.

Chapter 7:   Life is Yours!

"When you awake this morning, ask what you would do if this were your last day here…then do it!"

Glenn Wolkoff

"Life is what we make it, always has been, always will be."

Grandma Moses

"Everything comes to us that belongs to us if we create the capacity to receive it."

Rabindranath Tagore

If your life does not belong to you, then you have done something unwise along the path of your journey. I don't need to know you, to understand what it is you did. The answer is obvious, but yet, one of the most difficult life lessons to learn.

You did what many people do....

You took something simple and made it complicated!

The most important things in life are not material, yet we spend most of our life accumulating such things. What we need to accumulate is wisdom. We do that through our experiences. Learning our life lessons and evolving our spiritual self is what matters most.

You really only need three things in life to make you happy:

1. Love
2. Wisdom
3. Compassion

If you are going to pursue something in life, then first chase love. Love for others; love for yourself; and to be loved. It is more valuable than any material belonging you can imagine having.

Next, pursue wisdom, because you need wisdom to evolve and to recognize the truth. Without wisdom, you cannot learn the lessons life teaches you. Without wisdom, you cannot know truth. If you do not know truth, then you cannot know yourself.

Finally, you must have compassion for those who cannot find love or wisdom, because they need your help.

Love, wisdom, compassion and truth will keep your mind healthy and happy. Healthy minds know how to use free will to make wise decisions and to take wise actions. Healthy minds also allow you to stretch the limits of the physical as far as it can go.

Aristotle said, "The essence of the mind is the essence of life." A simple but profound statement. He was very wise.

Cary Grant said, "My formula for living is quite simple. I get up in the morning and I go to bed at night. In between, I occupy myself as best I can." Don't laugh, it makes sense.

Then we have Buddha who understood life, its goals, and its simplistic nature with the quote, "If we could see the miracle of a single flower clearly, our whole life would change."

So what does it really mean when I say life is yours?

There is an old saying that answers the question better than I can.

As we think, so we become!

You are the creator of your own life through your thoughts, your words, and your actions. Karma is created as you think those thoughts, speak those words, and take those actions. Each of us must find our own path to who we are and the life we live should be focused on getting there. So, where is it again that we are trying to go? We are going to where we can know our selves. These concepts are not complicated; however, we allow outside things to get in the way and change the course of our life.

The true course of mankind is to be who they are through an expression of their creativity. This will provide them with meaning and purpose in life. This will bring people together in productive relationships. This becomes what will make everyone happy.

Abraham Lincoln had it right when he said, "Whatever you are be a good one."

The basic process that should drive our lives is right thoughts, right words, and right actions based on wisdom and truth....your exercise of free will. This will also minimize your karmic debt. However, you are also free to not have the right thoughts, or not use the right words, or not take the right actions, and accumulate karmic debt. This happens because you do not choose to exercise your free will based on wisdom and truth. Not knowing truth makes one ignorant. Ignorance causes you to live a life of illusion. You must always act on truth and always speak the truth.

If you choose to let illusions drive your life, you will be steered away from wisdom and away from truth. The main cause of this behavior is a "condition" syndrome. You put a condition on your life that has not occurred as an excuse for not having what you want.

For example; if only I had met the right person....if only I had more money....if only I had more energy....if only I felt better....if only I had a bigger house....if only I had a better job....etc.

The condition syndrome occurs because (1) we don't want to take responsibility for where we are in life, and (2) we seek what we want by looking outside our self rather than turning inwards for answers. You need to be happy without any condition alibis in your life. If you are not, you will ultimately discover that having any or all of those things will not change your state of being.

Everything you need is here for you. You must open your eyes and see it. You must open your heart and experience it, and you must open your mind and visualize it. You need to be able to clearly see reality; things as they truly are; the truth.

When you chase illusions, you wander off your intended path and get lost. Once lost, you experience confusion, suffering, fear, anxiety, insecurity, and begin to feel powerless. Once you feel powerless, you stop using free will to choose your life because you now erroneously believe that life controls you.

This is how the simple becomes complicated. You allow it. You choose to let it happen.

If there is one lesson to be learned in life, it is this: understand that happiness in life is not achieved through the pursuit of material belongings. Instead of thinking, "I would be happy if I had more of something" think, "I am happy because I have things money can't buy." Make a list of those things. Be happy with what you have because as soon as you condition your happiness on what you do not have, you cannot be happy. Define your happiness on what you do not need because the truth is, the less you need, the richer you are.

I sometimes see things more clearly when I have a visual to picture rather than just reading words. Visualize the chart on the next page as your life and decide which side of the chart you would rather live on.

I would be happy if….	I am happy because….
I met the right person	I know many good people
I had more money	I have some money
I felt better	I am not ill
I had more energy	I use my energy wisely
I had a bigger house	I have a home
I had a better job	I have a job

Because your life becomes your state of mind, be aware of what you do, and be aware of why you do it. Always examine your motives. And most of all don't try to be like everyone else. You are you!

One of the most thought provoking statements I have read was written by Deepak Chopra. He said, "In my life nothing goes wrong. When things seem to not meet my expectations, I let go of how I think things should be. It's a matter of not having an attachment to any fixed outcome."

Intention:

Intention is more commonly defined as a course of action that one plans to follow. That is not the kind of intention I want you to focus on. I am talking about the higher consciousness of thinking.

To hold intent, you must call on the knowledge that exists in the consciousness of the Universe. Intent needs to be a thinking process whereupon you see what is coming before it arrives. Forming a picture in your mind of what it is you want, and then projecting the energy of that thought into the energy of the Universe. This is what creates and manifests reality.

There are a lot of books written on intent; however, you must understand what "deliberate intent" is if your goal is to create things. You can certainly change things and improve your life with the other thinking, but if creating things in the physical Universe is what you desire, you need to take a higher level approach.

Deliberate intent is the ability to see what does not exist. Traditional intent of a person's consciousness looks at an empty garden and sees an empty garden. Thoughts race through your mind of the need to buy seedlings or flowers, the need to plant, the need to grow something in this empty garden. This is an automatic thinking process for most of us. Deliberate intent would be to look at the empty garden and not see it as empty, but rather see everything you want in your garden as if it is really there. The challenge with the latter process of thinking is that it has to be automatic; completely free of any hesitation or doubt.

This higher consciousness thinking needs to become a firm belief in something for which there is no proof of reality. Complete trust in seeing what you want to exist, rather than what does. Traditional intent moves from thought to action to physical object. The intent I am talking about moves from thought directly to physical object. Your thought or intent **is** your action. Your intent becomes "thinking energy."

So, how does this really work? For the answer to make sense, you need to have a basic understanding of quantum mechanics. Higher consciousness intention creates an energy field of thought and information. Conscious energy is the source of all creation. The energy of the intention creates an image and projects that image into the energy of the Universe. The Universe contains all of the information necessary to create the image; to give the image form. Remember that the energy must be deliberate intent that is free from judgment and free from analysis. This level of intention is comparable to thought that occurs when you are dreaming.

The mind holds an image in thought of what it intends to create in the physical Universe. The energy of that intention connects with the energy of the consciousness in the physical Universe. Since everything is energy, including thoughts, intentions and information, you can actually direct the random energy in the Universe to take form. Tell the energy what to do. Tell the energy what to become. The energy is waiting to become organized matter through the powerful thought of your intention.

We have seven levels of energy in the body that are more commonly known as chakras or seals. The higher you move up through these energy levels, the more you can accomplish with your energy. The kind of creation we are discussing here requires your energy, your thoughts, and your intentions to be held in the highest or 7th level which is located at the crown of the head.

Truth:

In my first book _The Power_, I devoted an entire chapter to the subject of truth to reinforce the importance of using truth as a basis for making all of your choices in life. In a discussion of karma, truth is also important from a perspective of understanding truth and the relationship it has with your state of well-being. To be happy in life, you must have the ability to determine the truth or falsehood of something. So, what really is truth?

- ❖ We exist;
- ❖ The mind has the ability to know the truth through knowledge;
- ❖ Knowledge can only be obtained through experience;
- ❖ Therefore, truth is the relationship we experience between thoughts and objects.

Truth is often confused with belief. Belief has a subjective personal basis, while truth is an objective state. A belief may not be true. If I believe a diving board will support me and I walk out on the board and it collapses, then my belief was false. I could not know as a matter of truth that the diving board would support me. I believed it would.

Because we know truth through the experience of knowledge, can we acquire knowledge independent of experience? Yes; however, we cannot know if that knowledge is truth without experience. To validate knowledge, we must obtain it through experience based on our perceptual observations by the five senses. This is one of the main reasons we as spiritual beings love to live in the physical Universe. Our philosophies about life are experienced and validated through physical existence.

For truth to be known there must be some relationship to the actual physical state of things. Thomas Aquinas said, "A judgment is said to be true when it conforms to the external reality."

Logic is also an important aspect of obtaining truth, because logic is the mind's analytical ability to decipher information perceived.

One of the most interesting observations I have made in life is this: as difficult as it is to know truth, we sure spend a lot of our time trying to hide it.

"It is not who is right, but what is right, that is of importance."

---Thomas Huxley

Money:

One of the main distractions in life is money; acquiring money, spending money, investing money, and how not to lose our money. We invest a great deal of our time focused on money. It has often been said that money is the root of all evil. I don't agree with that because the true root of all evil has always been "ignorance." How you choose to deal with the subject of money is essential to your happiness in life. Having money can be a good thing; just remember to not let the pursuit of money control your life. Once you allow that to happen, you are on a path that can only lead you to unhappiness.

This is a good time to discuss my theory on money and how it relates to you becoming the person you want to be. Don't close the book when I say this:

"I believe that the monetary system in society needs to go away."

That's right. A Universe without money. Imagine that!

It's difficult to base your life on spiritual richness when mankind has created a society based on material richness. The fact is, we have created a Universe based on profit. Because of that, whether we have money or not determines much of the outcome of our lives. We have made money the most valuable resource in the Universe. The truth of the matter is that money is and will always be a method of controlling human behavior.

Money is a human creation, and the time has come to consider a new global thought process. I believe that you can escape the control of money by redirecting your priorities on non-monetary things in life. Even Albert Einstein said, "The most precious things in life are NOT those you get for money."

In reality, the concept of money is worthless.

The dilemma is that we have built a universal infrastructure that is focused and based on money. We have created a profit-driven Universe that has created profit- driven behavior. Money not only controls what we are entitled to, but also controls the thought process that defines who and what we are. Because man lives a life based on profit-driven behavior, our primary purpose in life has become self-preservation. When you are surrounded by a system of money and self-preservation, spiritual belief systems lose some of their meaning and understanding. After all, having an out of money experience is much easier than having an out of body experience.

Government and the financially rich preach that the purpose of money is to allow free trade of goods and services and to regulate the economy. I am suggesting that this is not the way life was ever meant to be. The most valuable asset of mankind is our ability to think, create, and use the resources provided to us. The pursuit of money interferes with this naturally intended process.

We need to consider changing the focus of our infrastructure from a money and profit base to a human resource based economy. Everyone has a role in life, and if everyone had the unlimited freedom to perfect that role, all of mankind's needs would be met. Mankind, through their human resources, would provide, produce and distribute all goods and services needed. Everyone would have free access to the necessities of life. This is how the Universe was meant to be. In essence, it is the ideal system of a "gift economy." A gift economy is where valuable goods and services are given on a regular basis without any expectation of any form of compensation. The practice of giving on a reoccurring basis among everyone in the community results in the circulation and distribution of all needed goods and services.

Earlier, I brought up the axiom of money being the root of all evil and I disagreed because I believe the true root of all evil is ignorance. I find it ironic that in today's society, a great portion of the population does not have access to education because they do not have enough money. The education of mankind is what allows us to develop our ability to think, create, and use the resources provided to us. Imagine the true cost to society for denying mankind access to education because they cannot financially afford it.

Today, the biggest single source driving social behavioral change is technology. Our behavior has been most impacted through the use of computers, cellular phones, and prescription drugs. And no surprise: technology is the basis of the most successful profit-driven products of this century.

Mankind can no longer afford to waste its time pursuing money. Those efforts need to be redirected to our own development. We need to be healthy, we need to be nourished, and we need to be educated. If we waste our minds, we have wasted a part of our existence. The cost of money has become too expensive. Wealthy is he who enjoys what he has!

The time is not yet upon us to live in a Universe of global cooperation with a free exchange of products and distribution. The time will eventually come upon us; there will be no choice.

Yeshua ben Joseph was compassionate when it came to the subject of money. A rare display of public frustration was triggered when merchants turned temple grounds into a marketplace. It was a place for people to help others in need. Instead, merchants and money changers were there to sell their goods and exploit others for profit. The message in his reaction was clear to me...how about you?

One other item worth noting about living in a Universe without a monetary system is that nearly all crime will be immediately eliminated.

Punishment:

Punishment is another concept that serves as a great distraction in life. It seems we have an unhealthy obsession with punishment. Life should not be about punishment and rewards; life is about learning your life lessons and being accountable for your behavior. Karma brings the balance of justice to everyone who requires it.

From the teachings of the Kabala, there is an ancient wisdom known as the "Sefirot." The Ten Sefirot contains divine emanations, or more commonly understood to be the divine energy or life force of existence. Of the ten concepts that describe the purpose of mankind, one of them is "Might" which is explained as having the power to restrain from not giving goodness to those who are unworthy, undeserving, or even those who will use your offer of goodness against you. I found this to be an interesting thought to appear on a list such as this. I cite the reference only to raise your awareness of the issue since it's appropriate for a discussion on punishment.

For those interested, I have briefly summarized the Ten Sefirot and their labels. Note that they are not in the order of significance as presented in the teachings of the Kabbalah, but rather grouped by subject matter for your convenience.

Might - Have the power to restrain from not giving goodness to those who are unworthy, undeserving, or even those who will use your offer of goodness against you.

Kindness - Have the desire to embrace and offer goodness to all

Victory - Have the power to overcome obstacles that stand in the way of goodness

Understanding - Have the ability to determine the truth or falsehood of something.

Wisdom - Have the power of intuitive insight.

Beauty - Have the discipline to allow for focused compassion.

Splendor - Have the power of determination, perseverance and deep inner commitment to realize one's life goals.

Kingdom - Have the power to express one's thoughts and emotions to others (self-expression.)

Foundation - Have the power to connect and communicate with outer-reality (the Earth.)

Crown - Reach the super-consciousness realm of experience.

Much of the global thinking in today's Universe is to punish those who act inappropriately. This makes people feel better. Much of the thought that consumes us on this issue is very negative and attracts negative energy. The required means to keep people out of society is also a very costly proposition. We all pay for it.

There are many ways to better correct inappropriate behavior, and that our thinking on this matter needs to change. Instead of being so focused on locking people up, our priority needs to focus on restoring victims to their status quo. I realize that not every action can present an opportunity to accomplish this. However, there are many that can.

Take for example the recent Ponzi scheme that defrauded thousands of investors of billions of dollars. Society applauded the apprehension, conviction, and locking away of the person responsible. We feel good that the person who defrauded these individuals will spend the rest of his life in jail. My question is, "How does this help the victims who lost everything they had?" If it were up to me, I would not put this person in jail. This individual was very smart and knew how to make money; unfortunately, his talents were misguided and used to harm others. Justice to me would be to have this person working hard, ten hours a day, seven days a week earning the money to pay back every penny to everyone he defrauded. This restores all of the victims to their original state of being.

It also provides a life lesson to the perpetrator…having to spend the rest of his life working hard and making lots of money, all of which he has to give away. What's more important; locking up wrongdoers or forcing them to restore the quality of life to their victims?

Also remember that true justice will always find a way to return to those who need it through the universal balancing of karmic debt.

Time:

Time is another great distraction in life. This is also another subject that I devote an entire chapter to in my first book *The Power*. As discussed in my first book, I believe that the concept of time is merely an illusion.

Time in the spiritual Universe does not exist; however, in the physical Universe time is necessary as a matter of reference and convenience so that we can function in physical life. The only true time that really exists in the physical universe is the present moment. That is where everything happens. Past moments are replaced by present moments, and future moments can only occur when they become present moments. Think of time as a sequence of events; events that can only take place in the present. Each event determines the next. Life is not about time; life is about choices and consequences that can only occur in one's present moment.

Clocks measure what time is defined to be; not what time is. The purpose of time was meant to be a measurement system of sequencing events. According to science, even life forms like photons have eliminated time from their existence. Photons live and die in the same instant because they travel at the speed of light. The speed of light eliminates time. Photons cannot experience time.

Time can really only be recognized through our conscious thought; therefore, it has no real significance in our physical existence. In the physical Universe, time is merely an illusion. In most cases, our thoughts of time serve as a great distraction in our life.

We never have enough time, and we always want more time; we stop doing things because it takes too much time; we don't finish things on time; we miss deadlines because of time, and on and on the list goes.

So, what if starting tomorrow, our concept of time was redefined. An hour was no longer 60 minutes, and 24 hours was only half a day. 1,000 days made a year instead of 365 days. There were 22 months in a year instead of 12. Those who thought they were 35 years old, are now only 20 years old. Do you start to see that none of this makes a difference? Time is a physical concept invented by mankind. We can redefine the rules whenever we want. If you were 35 years old and you suddenly found out that you are really only 20 years old, would you change how you view yourself? Would you feel younger? Would your health be better?

I often think that our physicality gets old and sick because we are programmed to die. We are taught that things happen at a certain age. We are taught that we can only live to a certain age. What if we were taught differently? All of this takes place based on a measurement system designed by us. Concentrate on events in your life. Understand that everything happens in the present.

Lose track of time!

Never forget that life is yours. Life belongs to you. Life is your creation. You create life through the choices you make. You are free to make choices no matter what happens to you. Make sure you use truth as the foundation of those choices. Most importantly, do not forget who you truly are. You are a spirit with a thinking mind. You are "thinking energy."

You come here to live in the physical Universe because you want to experience physicality. You are here to create. You are not here to destroy. You are here to do good for mankind and good for the Universe. Don't become lost in the maze of the human condition. Remember your purpose. Remember who you are.

Although your life is based on choices and their consequences, karma appears when you least expect it. Because you have been here before, there are consequences of past life choices. Your karma returns to you to balance the energies of your life. They only way to successfully get through your karmic tests, is to show the Universe that you have learned your life lessons and that you have evolved as a spiritual entity.

Good karma to all!

We have one life, and it is eternal. That one life as a spiritual being can be comprised of thousands of lives as a physical being. As a spiritual being, we choose to come into the physical Universe to experience life through the senses. We do this because as a spiritual being we do not have access to our senses; sight, sound, touch, taste and smell. We exist with or without our bodies. While in a physical body, we acquire knowledge through our experiences; we evolve through learning our life lessons; and we create through the consciousness of our mind. We come here because of our curious nature to experience the senses, and unfortunately, by entering the physical Universe, we also put ourselves at risk to experience disease, pain, suffering, and even death; all of which do not exist in the realm of spiritual life.

What people lose sight of is that once we accept physicality, we also accept responsibility for everything we think, everything we speak, and everything we do (or do not do.) All of these actions create energy in the Universe. All of the energy created begins a chain of consequences that will eventually find its way back to you. This is what karma is. Karma is a boomerang. Things happen to you because of something you have done. The key factor to understanding this concept is to remember that you cannot define the lifetime of things you have done by only your current physical incarnation. Karma does not always resolve things within the same physical incarnation that created the energy.

You may be doing everything right in your current physical life and you may be a wonderful person full of positive energy, and then something you consider awful, happens to you. You have not attracted that event through the laws of attraction. You have been delivered that event to learn a life lesson because of something you have done in a previous physical incarnation. Karma is the universal law of the Universe. Its purpose is to balance energies.

Remember; what happens to you in your life is not always rooted in the life you currently live. This is why you should never judge something that happens to you as good or bad, but rather ask yourself what lesson you are supposed to be learning because of it. Your spiritual self learns and evolves through the lessons it acquires in physical life, but only if you understand the intended lesson. Otherwise, the event continues to enter your life over and over again under many disguises.

With the creation of mankind there came an assumption that we act rational and make logical decisions. However; often we are self-defeating, irrational, and just plain foolish. We have become disinclined decision makers, justifying the path of least resistance.

Much of our life patterns are focused on money; how much of it we stand to gain and how much of it we stand to lose. Money decides what we can and cannot do, and we become out of balance with our natural intuitive thought processes. This causes us to be disconnected and unconcerned about our fellow man. For most of us, we are simply trying to survive.

Don't lose sight of the fact that the moments in your life are created by you; through your thoughts, your words, and the actions you take. Because these events become your life cycle, or karma, you are held responsible and accountable for them. If you do things right, you escape karmic debt. If you do things wrong, you must face the justice through your karmic debt cycle.

Do not focus on the outcomes in your life because they are not always in your control. Instead, focus on each act you take towards an expected outcome. Make sure it is the right thing to do, based on the knowledge and truth supporting your decision. This is how you accumulate wisdom.

Choices…choices…choices…life is all about free will!

Mankind needs to be an active participant and contributor to the Universe. Our role in life is to use our minds and creativity to produce and distribute what we all need. You create what you will receive. Your efforts and contribution is what creates the value for what you receive.

Mankind needs to create a consciousness of taking care of one another. Global production and voluntary distribution is what will take care of all mankind. Abundance in the Universe does exist. Unfortunately, the free will choices of greed, selfishness, and failure to love one another is what causes some to have what they need and others to not.

I often hear from people about how much they give to charity and think to myself, why is our focus not on ending the need for charity? The formula for mankind's success in this Universe is very simple, yet in the same breath, very complicated because of the infrastructure of the Universe we have created.

If we can at least all agree to four conditions in life, the Universe will begin to change in a positive direction:

1. Love yourself and others;
2. Forgive yourself and others;
3. Do no harm; and
4. Enable people to reach their greatest potential.

The Universe is our kingdom. We are responsible for creating the reality of our Universe. Mankind needs to step up and acknowledge their divine presence and the divine power that they were given. We have forgotten our divine nature. The time has come upon us to remember.

For those that continue to doubt the power of positive thought and positive energy, I ask that you find a time and a place to participate in what I call, "The Energy Circle."

It's a simple exercise. You will need a group of people; the more people, the stronger the impact. Each of you needs to search your mind for an experience you lived that was the happiest moment of your life. I want you to be able to close your eyes for one minute and visualize the experience over again. Experience it again! Relive it! Feel it! Bring everything you felt during that experience into your present moment. Now all join hands and form a circle, relax, take a deep breath, and close your eyes and spend a minute being in the happiest moment of your life. Have no expectations of anything that is supposed to happen. Simply, do it!

You already know that positive thought and positive energy has healing power over both your physical and spiritual state of being. The Energy Circle intensifies that power when positive thought and positive energy is united and shared among a group of people. Likewise, all mankind can experience this power through a positive global united consciousness.

I want mankind to experience the divinity it has! We need to understand that we are one large family that can alter the reality of the Universe we inhabit through a united and positive consciousness.

I will end my thoughts with a wonderful quote from Carl Sagan. "Somewhere something incredible is waiting to be known."

∞   Glenn

Buddha's Sutra

This body is not me.

I am not caught in this body.

I am life without boundaries.

I have never been born, and I shall never die.

Look at the ocean and the sky filled with stars;

manifestations of my wondrous true mind.

Since before time, I have been free.

Birth and death are only doors through which we pass;

sacred thresholds on our journey.

Birth and death are just a game of hide and seek.

So laugh with me, hold my hand, let us say goodbye,

only to meet again soon.

We meet today. We will meet again tomorrow.

We will meet at the source of every moment.

We will meet each other in all forms of life.

WOLKOFF MANIFESTO

Practice on a daily basis

- ❖ Live each day to the fullest!

- ❖ Do what makes you come alive!

- ❖ Live a life of purpose!

- ❖ Have a cause!

- ❖ Respect and love others!

- ❖ Respect and love yourself!

- ❖ Keep it simple!

- ❖ Be happy!

- ❖ Laugh often!

- ❖ Notice the beauty in yourself and in life!

- ❖ Use up all your talent!

- ❖ Enable the young to be participants!

- ❖ Success is doing and sharing what you love most!

www.ingramcontent.com/pod-product-compliance
Lightning Source LLC
Chambersburg PA
CBHW031602110426

42742CB00036B/687